First World War
and Army of Occupation
War Diary
France, Belgium and Germany

4 CAVALRY DIVISION
Divisional Troops
Royal Army Service Corps
Headquarters Divisional Army Service Corps (426
Company A.S.C.)
1 January 1917 - 31 January 1918

WO95/1158/9

The Naval & Military Press Ltd
www.nmarchive.com
Published in association with The National Archives

Published by

The Naval & Military Press Ltd

Unit 10 Ridgewood Industrial Park,

Uckfield, East Sussex,

TN22 5QE England

Tel: +44 (0) 1825 749494

www.naval-military-press.com

www.nmarchive.com

This diary has been reprinted in facsimile from the original. Any imperfections are inevitably reproduced and the quality may fall short of modern type and cartographic standards.

© **Crown Copyright**
Images reproduced by permission of The National Archives, London, England, 2015.

Contents

Document type	Place/Title	Date From	Date To
Heading	WO95/1158/9		
Heading	4 Cav Division Troops H.Q. 4 Cav. Div. ASC (426 Coy) 1917 Jan-1918 Jan		
War Diary	St Valery	01/01/1917	31/01/1917
Heading	War Diary of H.Q 4th Cavalry Divisional A.S.C. From February 1st 1917 To February 28th 1917 Volume II		
War Diary	St Valery	01/02/1917	28/02/1917
Heading	War Diary of H.Qrs. A.S. Corps. 4th Cavalry Division From 1-3-17 To 31-3-17		
War Diary	St Valery	01/03/1917	21/03/1917
War Diary	Rosemper	21/03/1917	21/03/1917
War Diary	Albert	22/03/1917	31/03/1917
Heading	War Diary H.Q. 4th Cavalry Divisional A.S.C. From 1-4-1917 To 30-4-1917		
War Diary	Aveluy	01/04/1917	05/04/1917
War Diary	Bihucourt.	06/04/1917	13/04/1917
War Diary	Marieux	14/04/1917	30/04/1917
Heading	War Diary of O.C., A.S.C., 4th Cavy Divin 9th May To 31st May 1917		
War Diary	Marieux	09/05/1917	14/05/1917
War Diary	Treux	15/05/1917	15/05/1917
War Diary	Bray	16/05/1917	16/05/1917
War Diary	Athies	17/05/1917	29/05/1917
Heading	War Diary of O.C., A.S.C., 4th Cavalry Division 4th June to 30th June 1917		
War Diary	Athies	04/06/1917	04/06/1917
War Diary	Sheet 62 C Q.1.a.	09/06/1917	30/06/1917
Heading	War Diary of O.C., A.S.C., 4th Cavalry Divin for the month of July 1917		
War Diary	Quaker Wood	03/07/1917	04/07/1917
War Diary	Athies.	05/07/1917	13/07/1917
War Diary	Villers-Carbonnel	14/07/1917	28/07/1917
Heading	War Diary H.Qrs. 4th Cavalry Divisional A.S. Corps August 1917		
War Diary	Villers Carbonnel	04/08/1917	18/08/1917
Heading	War Diary of O.C., A.S.C., 4th Cavy Divn for the month of September, 1917		
War Diary	Villers Carbonnel	13/09/1917	27/09/1917
Heading	War Diary of O.C., A.S.C. 4th Cavy Divn for the month of October, 1917		
War Diary	Villers Carbonnel	01/10/1917	23/10/1917
War Diary	Athies	10/11/1917	30/11/1917
Heading	War Diary of O.C., A.S.C. 4th Cavy Divn for December 1917		
War Diary	W. of Villers Faucon	01/12/1917	02/12/1917
War Diary	Athies	03/12/1917	28/12/1917
Heading	War Diary of H.Qrs. 4th Cavy Div. A.S.C for the month of January		
War Diary	Athies	01/01/1918	31/01/1918

WO 95/15879 A1

4 CAV. DIVISION TROOPS

H.Q. 4 CAV. DIV. A.S.C.
(426 COY)

~~Kitbag~~
~~1917 JAN~~ — 1918 JAN
1917 JAN

Army Form C. 2118

WAR DIARY
or
INTELLIGENCE SUMMARY
(Erase heading not required.)

89 COY ASC

Instructions regarding War Diaries and Intelligence Summaries are contained in F. S. Regs., Part II. and the Staff Manual respectively. Title Pages will be prepared in manuscript.

Place	Date	Hour	Summary of Events and Information	Remarks and references to Appendices
ST VALERY	1.1.19		Lieut Col Peterson returned from Hospital & resumed command	W1
	2.1.19		Routine	
	3		"	
	4		"	W?
	5		Q Battery R.H.A leave for ALLENVILLE lorries to 4 Cab troops S.C	
	6		Routine	
	7		"	
	8		"	W?
	9		"	
	10		Ambulance C.F.A to HALLOY lorries to 30 D.S.C	
	11		Wilson Prisoners Bn to Mondicourt lorries to 20 D.S.C	W?
	12		Purchase 1000 tons of to standing hard wood for fuel & cart out body of 30 Indians to common billing	
	13		Routine	W?
	14		½ Walbeck Prisoners Bn to WALLEN COURT lorries to 7 Cab troops S.C	
	15		Routine	W?
	16		½ Walbeck Prisoners Bn to WALLEN COURT	
	17		Routine	

1875 Wt. W593/826 1,000,000 4/15 J.B.C. & A. A.D.S.S./Forms/C. 2118.

Army Form C. 2118

WAR DIARY
or
INTELLIGENCE SUMMARY
(Erase heading not required.)

Instructions regarding War Diaries and Intelligence Summaries are contained in F.S. Regs., Part II. and the Staff Manual respectively. Title Pages will be prepared in manuscript.

Place	Date	Hour	Summary of Events and Information	Remarks and references to Appendices
Jerusalem	18.1.17		Submit new war establishment for A.T.C. supply & transport turned with the Division as there were too many supply men in this Division i.e. 88 as compared with 58 for a Postil Cavalry Division. Also 34 supply clerks are given as men of transport & being invalids or unless when the Division is on the move so they can only move with B echelon & could not stay with this supply officer who would be with this Bde & would not in able to reach them in time to issue. I also consider that all mounted officers will cavalry should have two horses in order that they can take their actions with them when moving with their Bde.	hu1
	19.1.17		Routine	hu1
	20.1.17		"	hu1
	21.1.17		"	
	22.1.17		"	
	23.1.17		"	
	24.1.17		Find that 90 Indian RaF can only eat & stab 2.5 tons of Gunwood in day. Also that issue ration of Bill Angles are much too light for this work. Purchase French holder Bill hole which are larger & heavier.	hu1
	25.1.17		Routine	
	26. "		"	hu1
	27. "		"	

Army Form C. 2118

WAR DIARY
or
INTELLIGENCE SUMMARY
(Erase heading not required.)

Instructions regarding War Diaries and Intelligence Summaries are contained in F. S. Regs., Part II. and the Staff Manual respectively. Title Pages will be prepared in manuscript.

Place	Date	Hour	Summary of Events and Information	Remarks and references to Appendices
ST VALERY	28.1.17		Routine	
	29 "		Routine	
	30 "		"	
	31 "		"	

Wilkinson
LT. COLONEL,
O.O. A.S.C. 4th CAVALRY DIVISION.

1875 Wt. W593/826 1,000,000 4/15 J.B.C. & A. A.D.S.S./Forms/C. 2118.

Serial No. 113.

Confidential

War Diary

of

H.Q. 4th Cavalry Divisional T.S.

From February 1st 1917 To February 28th 1917

Volume II

WAR DIARY or INTELLIGENCE SUMMARY

Army Form C. 2118

(Erase heading not required.)

Instructions regarding War Diaries and Intelligence Summaries are contained in F.S. Regs., Part II. and the Staff Manual respectively. Title Pages will be prepared in manuscript.

Place	Date	Hour	Summary of Events and Information	Remarks and references to Appendices
91. Valley	1.2.17		Routine finding listening posts in setile	
	2		" "	
	3		" "	
	4		" " Lt Rankin took over command of 2nd of R.P with 3rd Cav Div	
	5		" " 2/Lt Wells rejoins this Div	
	6		" "	
	7		" "	
	8		" "	
	9		" "	
	10		" "	
	11		" "	
	12		" "	
	13		" "	
	14		" "	
	15		" "	
	16		" "	
	17		Three above brought into force	
	18		" "	
	19		" " Lt Wood D.A.P struck off strength	
	20		Routine	
	21		" "	
	22		" "	
	23		" "	
	24		" "	
	25		" "	
	26		Routine Rankin Bde have Div Ammn	
	27		Routine work in a very bad state	
	28		" "	

Wilkinson Lt Col
O.C A.O.C 4th Cav Div

Serial No: 113.

CONFIDENTIAL

WAR DIARY

of

H. Qrs. A.S. Corps. 4TH. CAVALRY DIVISION

From 1-3-17   To. 31-3-17

WAR DIARY or INTELLIGENCE SUMMARY

Army Form C. 2118

(Erase heading not required.)

Instructions regarding War Diaries and Intelligence Summaries are contained in F.S. Regs., Part II. and the Staff Manual respectively. Title Pages will be prepared in manuscript.

Place	Date	Hour	Summary of Events and Information	Remarks and references to Appendices
St Valery	1.3.17	1	Purchased 100 tons of carrots at 20 francs 100 kilos for Remount.	
		2	All units drew from R.H. by M.T.	
		3	Forward march of officers & N.C.O. for Annexe	
		4	all surplus transferred nat[ive] work from Dis[trict] at last	
		5	A.D.S.T. Cavalry Corps indented dawn at Red Road	
		6	Find that 700 tons of forwarded cut by fatigue party likely to supply cattle [illegible] with horses Dis[trict] will make up 90 men can cut & stack 20 tons Cal. Rome came & turns same horses in Field Bank per day no calves informal & turns Cal. Road no end to purchase French Field Bank not for the work	
		7	horses came for supplies by B.H. Army and B.T.O. to Field manager order stopped to make refunds to grass stores for meeting ... that Dutch army. Rome was France in to cattle were	
		8	Rom[e] 10 horses of D.A.T. to Rome etc. Regim[en]t to collect cows employed [illegible] cavalry & allowing brought to a & continue for inspection Rome extracted on farmers farmer F.14.S. re charge 20 men from R Park & A.M.T. corp employed in cavalry from R.H. by M.T. find a [illegible] men drawing rations from A.M.T. Drought Rome cannot be sufficient on a lot of carts to ration for use of issued at France will not send Orb. Dis to inspect matters to 1.3. Col. & A.D.S.S F about it before	
		9		
		10		
		11	Routine	
		12	Col. A.D.V.S K authorises 3 lb of bran at 1/4 lb of Linseed extra for horses on Tr Park told A.D.V.S. From R Park & A.M.T Corp drawing rations from R.H. by M.T. about it & be informed use that A.D.V.S can authorise any rations as carriages are necessary	

1875. Wt. W593/826 1,000,000 4/15 J.B.C. & A. A.D.S.S./Forms/C. 2118.

WAR DIARY
or
INTELLIGENCE SUMMARY

(Erase heading not required.)

Army Form C. 2118

Place	Date	Hour	Summary of Events and Information	Remarks and references to Appendices
St Valery	13.3.17		Train orders only 7 days supplies are to be held in Reserve at B de dump	
"	14 "		Call O staff to lay down the strength of TS & Edbn	
	15		Routine seen ADST	
	16		Routine	
	17		Routine	
	18		Orders received at 12 m.m. for Div to move on 19.4. Webbit Queen from Fiennes Ion and out double wagons	
	19		march to St Riquier. Owen A.H.T. & R.Coll camp as bb of site up 8 am return for men & horses of Divl get rations	Before leaving
	20		march from St Riquier Owen to CAMACHES D.S.C ordered to demand rations as it is impossible for with little or no baggage, men their billets open to their own billets. Our motors to sent in factories to take over billets, but maintain an appropriate order in demand service & Royal Arts action to establish Confusion of Machengea about Frank after D.S.C. etc that but has nearly demanded.	
	21		B Eletton of Divisie Ammunition Carrie unable change of site & a at all wagons badly conducted & wagons with but horses very weak on many hills two Condition. Our HQ & relays take B Eletton at each ROSSIGNAL & motor lobe an at D.H.— Camp marked about 6 mile over 10 hours away to draw to double line all wagons on bad horses of mul & Arts	

Army Form C. 2118

WAR DIARY
or
INTELLIGENCE SUMMARY
(Erase heading not required.)

Instructions regarding War Diaries and Intelligence Summaries are contained in F. S. Regs., Part II. and the Staff Manual respectively. Title Pages will be prepared in manuscript.

Place	Date	Hour	Summary of Events and Information	Remarks and references to Appendices
ROBEMPRÉ	21/8/17		Batt. moves to leave at 10 am to Robempré to prepare to leave old Blanket waggons to first new Blanket waggons in exchange. Rolled it allowed to use extra hipsled to deliver to Robempré.	
Ollezy	22		Moved with 2/2 leave teams to Albert having passed new waggons in exchange of where old Div transfer used extra material supplied at 6 pm we were to unload. Refilled B Echelon to charge of Echelon warrant officer at Albert till 4.30 pm. Refit transport depot Rollet B Echelon warrant officer at Albert went on nubbin count.	
	23		Another B Echelon arrived. Report on unloading of B Echelon waggons & G.O.C. moving orders for an immediate Adv. Inspection ran TD 597 6 Aug	
	24		Rec'd Rd for horse lines waggons find that will not cover with loading about 2½ tons of kit waggons on this waggon some where looked up on this	
	25		Visit H.P. of Richmen Rds find that they are Swing fed on new rations by orders of Ch.Q.. and it [illegible] rations to the App Rds & is not under Div for administration arrange to and from AVELUY by road from AVELUY	
	26		Railhead changed to AVELUY	
	27		Routine	
	28		Routine	

WAR DIARY
or
INTELLIGENCE SUMMARY

(Erase heading not required.)

Army Form C. 2118

Place	Date	Hour	Summary of Events and Information	Remarks and references to Appendices
AUBERT	30.3.17		Routine	
	31."		Divisional Horse Shows slipped Horseshoes were sent back about 18 miles from the front line. ADDVS 6 Cavalry tested horses shod with the clipping of removable fit a nail. It was noticed that horses shod with ordinary shoes did not suffer as much from slipping. As no horses were accustomed to shoes of new pattern & as they had in all cases been left to be shod from time in the rough & some of course in the soft, going in the country over it's heavy rising, few hits in refixing horses going over it.	

W. Whitmore
LT. COLONEL
O.C. A.S.C. 4th CAVALRY DIVISION

Serial No: 113.

WAR DIARY

H.Q. 4TH CAVALRY DIVISIONAL A.S.C.

FROM 1-4-1917 TO 30-4-1917.

WAR DIARY

INTELLIGENCE SUMMARY
(Erase heading not required.)

Army Form C. 2118

HQ 4TH. CAVALRY. DIV. A.S.C.

Place	Date	Hour	Summary of Events and Information	Remarks and references to Appendices
AVELUY	1.4.17		Rations AVELUY S/H Stks. attached to AHT Coy for duty	
"	2.4.17		Routine	
"	3.4.17		Rations moved to MIRAUMONT supplies for am Bde & S/H troops delivered by M.T.	
"	4.4.17		Routine	
"	5.4.17		Attached 2/Lt W.D. WELLS, 60 Dro 7710 mules from 4 to Res. Park to 10th Res. Park for temporary duty.	
Bihucourt	6.4.17		Marched via BAPAUME to G.17.d. E. of BIHUCOURT. Traffic very heavy on main ALBERT- BAPAUME Road. Res. Park loaded up at MIRAUMONT Rns. with 72,960 lbs Oats. Res. hay Res'res Park loaded up at again. weather extremely severe - high wind, snow. Animals suffering from exposure.	
"	7.4.17		Routine.	
"	8.4.17		Routine.	
"	9.4.17		No. I Section D.S.C. brought up & parked between BEHAGNIES & SAPIGNIES	
"	10.4.17		Rns. moved up to ACHIET-LE-GRAND. Bst & Res. Park moved on to MORY in the morning, but withdrew it again to BIHUCOURT same evening.	
"	11.4.17			
"	12.4.17		Routine - animals still suffering from severity of weather. Majority of casualties no less amongst clipped mules - unclipped mis stand the cold much better.	

Army Form C. 2118

WAR DIARY
or
INTELLIGENCE SUMMARY   Page II
(Erase heading not required.)

Place	Date	Hour	Summary of Events and Information	Remarks and references to Appendices
BIHUCOURT	13.4.17	—	No.I Section A.S.C. - WORKSHOP - 4 to Rev. Park + Det. 10 to Rev. Park withdrawn to ALBERT. Got animals into covered stabling, most very exhausted.	
	14.4.17	—	Railhead ALBERT - Marched to billets in MARIEUX - A.H.T. Co.	
MARIEUX	15.4.17		VAUCHELLES. Routine.	
"	16.4.17		"	
"	17.4.17		"	
"	18.4.17		Inspected all A.S.C. units. Submitted organization for a Tram to be used when M.T. fails. Saw G.O.C.	
"	19.4.17		Capt. Brown joins from B.T.O. Lucknow B.A.C. takes over duties as Adjutant vice Lt Knipell to H.P.	
"	20.4.17	—	Arrived to hand back all from returns to Res Park.	
"	21.4.17		Saw D.D.S+T.V. Army - Attended conference on horses.	
"	22.4.17		Routine.	
"	23.4.17		Inspected both Reserve Parks.	
"	24.4.17		Inspected A.H.T. Co.	
"	25.4.17		SIALKOT R BDE. moved back from AVELUY to this Area, also both Res. Parks to DOULLENS.	

Army Form C. 2118

WAR DIARY
or
INTELLIGENCE SUMMARY
(Erase heading not required.)

Place	Date	Hour	Summary of Events and Information	Remarks and references to Appendices
MARIEUX	26.11.17		No. I Section D.S.C. moved here from ALBERT. Rhd. BELLS 5QWISE	
"	27.11.17		Routine - Inspected Rho. Parks. 4 A.H.T. Co.	
"	28.11.17		Routine - A.H.T. Co. move to join Rho. Parks at DOULLENS.	
"	29.11.17		Routine	
"	30.11.17		Routine	

NWhitmore Lt Col
O.C. A.O.C. 4th Corps Dis

Confidential

Serial No. 113.

War Diary
of
O.C. A.S.C. 4th Cavy Divn

9th May to 31st May 1917

WAR DIARY or INTELLIGENCE SUMMARY

Army Form C 2118.

MAY 1917.

Place	Date	Hour	Summary of Events and Information	Remarks and references to Appendices
MARIEUX	9th		Took over charge from Lieut Col. G.L. PETERSON, who left at 7 p.m. to report to O.C. 32th Divisional Train. Lieut J.A. Heymann A.S.C. joined A.H.T.Co.	
"	10th		3d Squadron with 1 waggon A.H.T.Co. marched to MEAULTE. Interned D.S.T. ALBERT rearranged for 8 G.S.W. from B/MS. to join their unit. 16th Bde R.H.A. less "A" Battery moved from V Corps. to LE TRANSLOY	
"	11th		Escort Sqdn. K.D.G. rejoined Regt. LOUVENCOURT from Cav. Corps. H.Q. Field Squadron R.E. marching to BRIE. Thin Rhd. to-day PERONNE. 49 O.R. 7 Sgdm + 1 B.O. 500.R. of Sialkoth Bde. proceed to MEAULTE to-day to join their etc. for new Area.	
"	12th		Divisional Amm. Park move to MARIEUX	
"	14th		A.H.T.Co — 4 4th Cav. Res. Park, Nos 4 Sects 10th R. Park marched to AVELUY.	
TREUX	15th "		Divisional HdQrs. moved to TREUX N° 1 Sect. D.S.C. " O 2nd L Sect 6th C N° 2 " " " " PROYART	
BRAY	16th "		Divisional H.Q. moved to BRAY — Thier H.T. units to FRISE	

Army Form C. 2118.

WAR DIARY
or
INTELLIGENCE SUMMARY.
MAY 1917

(Erase heading not required.)

Place	Date	Hour	Summary of Events and Information	Remarks and references to Appendices
ATHIES	17th		Divisional H.Q. marched to ATHIES. Am. Park to CAVIGNOLLES. 3 H.T. Units to do. MONS-EN-CHAUSSÉE	
do.	22nd		Nos 1 & 2 Sections D.S.C. moved in to MONS-EN-CHAUSSÉE	
do.	29/6		Ammunition Park to ¼ mile E. of FOUCACOURT.	

M. Sant
LT. COLONEL,
O.C. A.S.C. 4th CAVALRY DIVISION.

Confidential

Maj. Durrs.

O.C., A.S.C., 4th Cavalry Division

4th June to 30th June 1917.

Army Form C. 2118.

WAR DIARY
~~INTELLIGENCE SUMMARY~~
(Erase heading not required.)

JUNE 1917

Place	Date	Hour	Summary of Events and Information	Remarks and references to Appendices
ATHIES	4th		D.H.Q. (Rear report centre) moved to Wood Q.I.A. Sheet 62.C.	
			LOCKNOW Bde. (less trench party) moved to ST. CHRIST area.	
			MHOW Bde. (less trench party) moved to HAMELET area.	
			LOCKNOW Bde. H.Q. moved from ST. CHRIST to ATHIES.	
Sheet 62.C. Q.I.A.	9th		B.S.O. Sialkote Bde. received return of S.O. Dismounted Bde. vice Capt. A. RICHARDS returned to MHOW Bde.	
	17th		MHOW Bde. (less trench party) moved to ENNEMAIN area.	
			SIALKOTE Bde. (less trench party) ———— HAMELET ————	
	19th		A.H.T. Co. received 55 Remounts.	
			CAPT. R. RANKIN from 4 Cav. Res. Park to B.T.O. Sialkote Bde.	
			CAPT. J.N. WAUGH ———— B.T.O. Sialkote Bde. to 4 Cav. Res. Park.	
	21st		4 Cav. Res. Park received 58 Remounts.	
	24th		Absorption of No 6 Sect No.10 Res. Park into 4 Cav. Res. Park completed.	
	25th		LIEUT. J.O. PHILIPPS from H.Q. ASC. to 4 Cav. Res. Park.	
			LIEUT. A. HENDERSON from 4 Cav. Res. Park to H.Q. A.S.C.	
	30th		LOCKNOW Bde. from ST. CHRIST to HAMELET Area.	
			SIALKOTE Bde. from HAMELET to ST. CHRIST area.	110M↑ Lt. Col. Commdg. A.S.C. 4th Cav. Dn.

Serial No: 113.

Confidential

War Diary
of
O.C., S.C., 2nd Cavalry Divn
for the month of July, 1917

Army Form C. 2118.

WAR DIARY
of J.A.C. Wolfe
4th Cavalry Division

INTELLIGENCE SUMMARY. July /17.
(Erase heading not required.)

Instructions regarding War Diaries and Intelligence Summaries are contained in F. S. Regs., Part II. and the Staff Manual respectively. Title pages will be prepared in manuscript.

Place	Date	Hour	Summary of Events and Information	Remarks and references to Appendices
QUAKER WOOD	3rd		2/Lieut. A.H. Mills D.S.C. invalided to England & struck off strength.	
	4th		D.H.Q. moved back to ATHIES.	
ATHIES	5th		2/Lieut. F.C. Begg rejoined Amm. Park from H.P. W.E. 533 – new Establishment for Divisional Supply Column in lieu of a reduction of ;- Road Officers 1 ; M.T. Drivers 8 ;- Batmen 2, on previous Establishment.	
	6th		2/Lieut. H. to Frank A.S.C. arrived reported to Div. Supply Column from M.T. School ST. OMER.	
	8th		Div. Amm. Park moved to LE MESNIL.	
	9th		No 4 Cav. Div. Park moved to MONS.	
	13th		D.H.Q. moved to VILLERS- CARBONNEL	
VILLERS- CARBONNEL	10th		34 G.S.W. under Lt. J.O. Phillips from Div Park & MAIREPAS for Salvage Duties.	
	14th		20 G.S.W. under 2/Lt E. Evans from Div Park to LONGUEAU for Duty under Central Purchasing Board	
	19th		T/2/Lt J.A. Heyman attd Aux. M.T.C. invalided to ENGLAND.	

Army Form C. 2118.

WAR DIARY
or
INTELLIGENCE SUMMARY.
(Erase heading not required.)

Instructions regarding War Diaries and Intelligence Summaries are contained in F. S. Regs., Part II. and the Staff Manual respectively. Title pages will be prepared in manuscript.

Place	Date	Hour	Summary of Events and Information	Remarks and references to Appendices
VILLERS-CARBONNEL	19th (cont) 28th		2/Lieut. J. McN. KELLY from Base A.S.C. Depot to A.H.T. Co. Lt. Col. R. E. SANDERS proceeds on evacuation leave to U.K. C.R.Brown Capt. for Asst. D.O.C. A.S.C. 4th Corps.	

Serial No: 113

War Diary

I.G.C. 4th Cavalry Divisional. W/Shops

August 1917.

Army Form C. 2118.

WAR DIARY
of
INTELLIGENCE SUMMARY.
(Erase heading not required.)

Instructions regarding War Diaries and Intelligence Summaries are contained in F.S. Regs., Part II and the Staff Manual respectively. Title pages will be prepared in manuscript.

H.Q. 4TH CAVALRY DIV. ASC
August 1917

Place	Date	Hour	Summary of Events and Information	Remarks and references to Appendices
VILLERS CARBONNEL	4.8.1917		No 1 Section of 4th Cav Supply Column rejoined from Detached Duties at AMIENS	
	6.8.1917		2nd Lieut E P RIVAZ with 20 O.R. Wagons 4th Cav Reserve Park on Detached Duties arrived back in this unit	
	9th	-	2nd Lieut T R RIDPATH Divisional Supply Column returned his report to M.S. Corps Supply Park to do duty with 293 Sleep Battery	
	15th	-	Capt. W H RAYNER R.A.M.C. arrived with Divisional Supply Column Lieut F H HURST U.S.M.C. transferred to 5th North Cavalry Field Ambulance Notification received that Capt M G W BURTON M.C. Divisional Supply Column was being returned at time for duty G.H.Q. Lieut J M C BARNETT returned to report to M 1st Corps Troops Supply Column	

Wilson Lt Col
Commdg A.S.C. 4th Cavalry Division

Confidential

Serial No. 113.

War Diary
of
O.C., A.S.C., 4th Cavy Divn.
For the month of September, 1917.

Army Form C. 2118.

WAR DIARY
or
INTELLIGENCE SUMMARY.
(Erase heading not required.)

H.Q. 4TH CAVALRY DIV= A.S.C.

SEPTEMBER 1917

Instructions regarding War Diaries and Intelligence Summaries are contained in F. S. Regs., Part II. and the Staff Manual respectively. Title pages will be prepared in manuscript.

Place	Date	Hour	Summary of Events and Information	Remarks and references to Appendices
VILLERS CARBONNEL	13-9-17		War Establishment of Mob: Ammunition Park & Supply Column reduced by motor Cars and 2 motor Cycles. A.O.S.T. Cavalry Corps T/895 B/10-9-17.	
	18-9-17		↑ Lieutenant A.M. BEATSON A.S.C. left Supply Column on transfer to 1st R.C. Repair Shop, PARIS.	
	19-9-17		↑ Lieut A. HENDERSON A.S.C. transferred from 4th Cavalry Div: R.C. to 4th Cavalry Reserve Park.	
	26-9-17		Establishment of London resi Supply Column reduced by 20 (10 in each Section) A.O.S.T. Cav Corps M1500/2 D/3 and 23-9-17	
	27-9-17		↑ Lieutenant T. ROGERS A.S.C. from 4th Cavalry Div: R.C. to England with orders to report to O.C. N°2 School Electros School, BEDFORD on 20-10-17.	

M_____
H.Col
O.C. A.S.C. 4th Cavalry Division

Confidential

War Diary
of
O.C., R.L.C. with Cavy Divn
for the month of October, 1917.

113.

Army Form C. 2118.

WAR DIARY
or
INTELLIGENCE SUMMARY.   October /17.
(Erase heading not required.)

Instructions regarding War Diaries and Intelligence Summaries are contained in F.S. Regs., Part II. and the Staff Manual respectively. Title pages will be prepared in manuscript.

Place	Date	Hour	Summary of Events and Information	Remarks and references to Appendices
VILLERS CARBONNEL	1st	—	50 Drivers, Category A, left R.R. for Base, on being replaced by same number from lower category.	
do	4th	—	D. Amm. Park moved to P27A Central Sheet 62C.	
—	20th	—	Capt. A.M. HOWARD, O.C. D. Amm. Park with 2/Lt. H.G.W. BUSBRIDGE 15 O.R's left the Amm Park to report to Commandant Abbeville — Authority Cav. Corps Q 2888 B/16.10.17. CAPT. H.R. HOWARD assumed command o/c A.P.	
—	22nd	—	50 lorries from D.S. Col. 2 Cav. Dn. attached to this Division & locate at ESTREES for work in connection with Cavalry Corps Shuttings Scheme etc	
—	23rd	—	50 lorries from D.S.C. 3rd Cav. Dn. attached to this Division for the same purpose Located at MONS 4th Cav Amm. Park ceased to be No.79 Coy. M.T. A.S.C. Authority A.D.S.T. Cav. Corps. M/1500/42	

C.R. Brown Capt for
LT. COLONEL,
O.C. A.S.C. 4th CAVALRY DIVISION.

WAR DIARY

INTELLIGENCE SUMMARY.
(Erase heading not required.)

H.Q 4th Coy Divl A.S.C

November 17

Army Form C. 2118.

Place	Date	Hour	Summary of Events and Information	Remarks and references to Appendices
ATHIES	10	7ᵃ	Hd Qrs A.S.C moved with D.H.Q from VILLERS CARBONNEL to ATHIES	
	13	7ᵖ	62 Coy "B" men arrived from Base	
	15	7ᵃ	43 G.S. Wagons of A.H.T Coy sent to QUINCONCE to load up with ammunition	
			60 Division Coy "A" men sent to Base	
	19	6ᵖ	Completed issue of 10th Rations to see units of the Division	
	20	4ᵃ	Supply Column left MONS-EN-CHAUSSÉE and proceeded to RANCOURT	
			Heavy Section Reserve Park moved to near DEVISA	
	21	5ᵖ	A.H.T Coy moved into ATHIES	
			Light Section Reserve Park marched to FINS	
			Railhead changed from PERONNE LA CHAPELETTE to YTRES	
	22	7ᵖ	Light Section Reserve Park dumped loads at FINS and proceeded to GOUZEAUCOURT	
			for duty with 3rd Bde Tanks	
	23	3ᵖ	Hd Qrs A.S.C returned to ATHIES with D.H.Q	
			A.H.T Coy returned to MONS-EN-CHAUSSÉE	
			Railhead BRIE	
	24	4ᵃ	Light Section Reserve Park working with 3rd Bde Tanks	

Army Form C. 2118.

WAR DIARY
or
INTELLIGENCE SUMMARY.
(Erase heading not required.)

November 17

Instructions regarding War Diaries and Intelligence Summaries are contained in F. S. Regs., Part II. and the Staff Manual respectively. Title pages will be prepared in manuscript.

Place	Date	Hour	Summary of Events and Information	Remarks and references to Appendices
ATHIES.	25th		VILLERS FAUCON	
			HdQrs A.S.C. moved with D.H.Q. to Villers Faucon from Athies to ATHIES	
	26th			
	27th		Light section Reserve Park working with Sanits	
	28&30th			
	29th		A.H.T Coy returned ammunition to QUINCONCE	
			Railhead changed from BRIE to PERONNE-LA-CHAPELETTE	
	30th		Hd Qrs A.S.C. moved with D.H.Q. to VILLERS FAUCON.	

H. Marshall
for LT. COLONEL.
O.C. A. & O. 4th CAVALRY DIVISION.

Confidential

War Diary
of
O.C, A.S.C. 4th Cav Divn
for December 1917

Army Form C. 2118

113

WAR DIARY
or
INTELLIGENCE SUMMARY
(Erase heading not required.)

H.Q. A.S.C. 4th Cav. Div. DECEMBER 1918

Place	Date	Hour	Summary of Events and Information	Remarks and references to Appendices
W. of VILLERS FAUCON	1st	—	Division in action. Ordered Light Section R.P. to join Heavy Section at E.14.b (Sheet 62 c) from TRESCAULT Area. Railhead CHAPELLETTE. — D.S.C. moved to PROYART.	
do.	2nd	—	Railhead moved to LA FLAQUE. — Division still in action. LIEUT. J.L. TREDOR PT. admitted to F.P.	
ATHIES	3rd	—	Division returned to old camp in ATHIES. R.P. returned to MONS-EN-CHAUSSÉE.	
do.	7th	—	Railhead moved to PERONNE, CHAPELLETTE.	
do.	9th	—	THAW Scheme came into operation	
do.	10th	—	to	
do.	11th	—	continued.	
do.	12th	—	CAPT. F.H. MOSELEY Evacuated to F.P. — LIEUT. W.D. WELLS Rejoined from F.P. to Div. Ammunition Park, amalgamated with D.S.C. under command D.A.D.S.C.: including 33 lorries, 2 cars & 5 motorcycles.	
do.	13th	—	2/Lieut. A.L. Lloyd joined from 1st Cavalry Division, & attached to B.S.C. Luckmow Bde. for instruction.	
do.	17th	—	T/Lieut. J.F.B. ASHTON Evacuated to F.P. Heavy snow.	

Army Form C. 2118

WAR DIARY
or
INTELLIGENCE SUMMARY
(Erase heading not required.)

Instructions regarding War Diaries and Intelligence Summaries are contained in F.S. Regs., Part II. and the Staff Manual respectively. Title Pages will be prepared in manuscript.

Place	Date	Hour	Summary of Events and Information	Remarks and references to Appendices
HQrs. ATH IES	20th		CAPT. R. RANKIN reported invalided to ENGLAND & struck off strength on 5-12-17. 22° foot rendered.	
do.	21st		CAPT. W.H. SEALY admitted to H.	
do.	23rd		2/Lieut S.C.G. FIELDER reported from Base Depot HAVRE, former posted to Supply Column, latter B.T.O. Sialkot Bde. vice Capt. R. Rankin struck off strength.	
do.	26th		MAJOR E.W. BAGNELL sent to BASE, under medical certificate as being unfit for further duty at the front.	

[signature]
LT. COLONEL,
O.C. A. & O. 4th CAVALRY DIVISION.

1875 Wt. W593/826 1,000,000 4/15 J.B.C. & A. A.D.S.S./Forms/C. 2118.

War Diary
of
Afr. I.b. Coy Sirie A.I.F.
for the
month of January.

Army Form C. 2118.

WAR DIARY
or
INTELLIGENCE SUMMARY.
(Erase heading not required.)

JANUARY 1918.

Place	Date	Hour	Summary of Events and Information	Remarks and references to Appendices
ATHIES	1st		Lt. BRUCE-MAJOR from Reserve Park, proceeded to join 3 Rde. Tank Corps	
	2nd		2 Lt. J.W. FRANK rejoined Supply Column from P.	
	6th		CAPT. J.R. GALBRAITH, O/C Column Workshops proceeded to 1st Base M.T. Depot as medically unfit for service in forward area. Car Corps A5502 g 4/S.	
	7th		THAW SCHEME in force at 6 p.m. but cancelled at 7.30 p.m.	
	10th		Lt. J.P.B. ASHTON returned to duty with DSC from P.	
	11th		Thaw Scheme came into force at midnight 11/12.	
	12th		2 Lt. S.G.G. FIELDER transferred from D.S.C. to Aux. H.T.C. Thaw Scheme in force – All lorries withdrawn.	
	13th		do.	
	14th		Thaw Scheme discontinued – Usual supplies, also the 2 days Dump formed at Rhd. during Thaw Scheme cleared by M.T. 2nd TOLLER, Reserve Park run over killed by Ambulance.	
	15th		Thaw Scheme in force at 6 p.m.	
	16th		do. All lorries withdrawn. 50 Category "B" men arrived for Reserve Park from Base	

Army Form C. 2118.

WAR DIARY
or
INTELLIGENCE SUMMARY.
(Erase heading not required.)

JANUARY 1918.

Place	Date	Hour	Summary of Events and Information	Remarks and references to Appendices
ATHIES.	17th		Thaw Scheme continued	
	18th		do. do. 50 Catgors. A Driver dispatched to Braw from Reserve Park.	
	19th		Thaw Scheme continued (4th day) NO lorries	
	20th		do. do. Special permission obtained r 22 lorries sent to draw Coal wood & conveyed to Brigades	
	21/50		Thaw Scheme cancelled at 6 p.m. (6th day) Amm. Section of D.S.C. work from ESTREES to ETERPIGNY.	
	26th		MAJOR H.D. CHAPLIN reported for duty & assumed command of Reserve Park.	
	31/50		Inspected Amm. H.T. Co.	

C.F. Browne .... LT. COLONEL,
O.C. A.S.C. 4th CAVALRY DIVISION.

www.ingramcontent.com/pod-product-compliance
Lightning Source LLC
Chambersburg PA
CBHW081248170426
43191CB00037B/2079